INSTEAD OF SADNESS

In Catherine Abbey Hodges' *Instead of Sadness* the beauty is there as the bread of life, as the poems enter and grow in us—the kind of experience we come to expect in good poems—the feeling of "Ah yes, that's right." In classically beautiful and precise language, we are reminded again and again of what we didn't know we knew. They effect their changes in us subtly and steadily, convincing us that their perceptions and discoveries are our own—which, when we have given them our full attention, is exactly right. In the course of discovering her own experience in the unfolding of the poem she lets us in on the adventure; we believe we are experiencing her surprise at the poem's destination just as she is discovering it. And we know, at that moment, that we are the better for it. These are truly beautiful, finely honed poems.

—Dan Gerber, author of *Sailing through Cassiopeia*

Catherine Abbey Hodges' *Instead of Sadness* is a book to savor. One can't rush through these poems; they're not built for speed. They arrive on the page without waste, in language that is intimate and transparent. At times they come at you from an unusual angle—not the expected poem about flowers, for example, but one about their stems. And some of her poems are relatively short, holding up to the light a passing moment or two. But to paraphrase one of her metaphors: word, phrase, poem, each should "carry something larger than itself / without swaggering." And that's the beauty of her work. Calm and meditative, lyrical, structured more by the shift of images than by events, her poems carry a human and spiritual resonance of what is "signed and wondrous" long after they close.

—Peter Everwine, author of *Listening Long and Late*

Instead of sadness, what does Catherine Abbey Hodges offer us in her latest collection of poems? Wonder. Reverence. An embrace of polarities. She offers us—inside each musical line, within each vibrant trope—a luminous wisdom. Each poem gives us an arresting bit of the world, its "jumbled / life: shabby, incandescent." Each poem gives us a world "replenished like a well // in blues and greens and wings." Nuanced, deeply lyrical, Hodges' work moves us in ways that call us to be more human, more humane. That her poems are alive and making their way in our world is cause for much grateful celebration.

—Paulann Petersen, Oregon Poet Laureate Emeritus

INSTEAD OF SADNESS

POEMS

CATHERINE ABBEY HODGES

Richard —
There are no words
for my gratitude
o astonishment.

GUNPOWDER PRESS • SANTA BARBARA
2015

Thank you for your
careful, deep reading.
love,
Catherine Abbey
Hodges

3 March 2016

Published by Gunpowder Press
David Starkey, Editor
PO Box 60035
Santa Barbara, CA 93160-0035

Cover photo: Catherine Abbey Hodges
Back cover photo: Clara Hodges
ISBN-13: 978-0-9916651-7-4

www.gunpowderpress.com

For Donna Burns Alderson Abbey

ACKNOWLEDGEMENTS

Grateful acknowledgement is made to the editors of the following publications, in which these poems or earlier versions of them appeared:

All the While (Finishing Line Press): "Between Shores," "Button Weather," "Dark and Late," "Everything Important" and "Safe"

Askew: "Homage to Old Books and Childhood," "Instead of Sadness," "Legends of Quick" and "Turned Sparrow"

Christian Century: "True and Useful"

Cider Press Review: "Our Lady of Betwixt"

Connotation Press: An Online Artifact: "January Song," "Polaris" and "South of Cayucos"

The Cresset: "Something to Fill"

Into the Teeth of the Wind: "Stems"

Oberon: "How to Begin"

Rock and Sling: "Guilty of Dust"

The Southern Review: "An Algebra of Fifty" and "Another Country"

String Poet: "Anniversary"

Tar River Poetry: "Beach Bone," "Couch on the Beach" and "October, Ellensburg"

"An Algebra of Fifty" also appeared in *Verse Daily*

"Guilty of Dust," "Stems" and "True and Useful" also appeared in *All the While* (Finishing Line Press)

"Safe" also appeared in *The Heart of All There Is: Reflections on Home* (Holy Cow! Press)

Contents

— switch

(purple) *ottom*

I.

In the Scriptorium

When I look up from the gold leaf,
the brush of two hairs, the milky vellum,
the Crusades have begun.

The holy family, fleeing through the arc
of the O beneath my hand—I swear
I see them look back, hear

the small child cry out, see the mother
cast her harrowed eyes upward,
then straight at me.

October, Ellensburg

Evening sky blooms roses
while a rusty needle stitches landscape
to shifting heaven.

Nothing is only one thing.

In a lit window south of town
a woman peels carrots, each orange curl
a word on the wet counter.

In liminal works the simple
words ~~Eth~~ ~~I~~ ~~infinitude~~
~~Are~~ ~~the~~ keys that open Will
infinitude

Stems

Lately I catch myself
less interested
in flowers
than what precedes them:
those leggy necks
ribbed and weaving
wandering skyward
hilariously furred
    or thorny or sinewed or silken
metaphorical as serpents
durable as doves
monastic
capacious
muscular and umbilical
as drinking straws
as question marks
submerged in molten earth
delivering answers
that look for all the world
like cornflowers.

[handwritten annotation: poetry vs. prose]

[handwritten annotation: the mind works this or to UR]

15

Intro to Lit

I got no use for words
said Gil's dad a long time
before the summer Gil was my student,
but those are words that stay
with you a long time.

That summer the bees began to go missing.
Ernie, who most days sat in front of Gil,
said he didn't much mind.
I got no use for bees Ernie said
on a sweaty break

between simile and metaphor—
as a kid in Modesto he'd been stung all over
by a swarm of bees another boy
had knocked out of a tree.
All over my face and arms, my bare stomach.

That was the day Gil told me
on the way to the parking lot
what his dad had said. *But I needed his words*
Gil said. *I sure's hell had a use for them.*
Asphalt mirage-pools

shimmered with students, poplars,
pick-ups. Gil said Ernie's bees
made him want to cry like a good poem.
Like this he said, surprised, touching
his face. *Like this right now.*

Polaris

Bees work the vetch, moths tryst
in the jasmine, and on it turns, the world
replenished like a well

in blues and greens and wings while leaves
like needles, minnows, hosts, hands
conjure oxygen.

Near the center of each nasturtium leaf
a north star. Here the heavens
pivot, certain engines catch.

Reprise

Spices

How like a death the whole sky now,
now sky's a twined idea of forever
as you said last week of a Bach fugue.

How like forever today's drowned leaves
this autumn lake steaming with spices
from far groves, distant kitchens.

How to Begin

Wipe the crumbs off the counter.
Find the foxtail in the ear of the old cat.
Work it free. Step into your ribcage.

Feel the draft of your heart's doors
as they open and close. Hidden latches
cool in your hand.

Hear your marrow keep silence,
your blood sing. Finch-talk
in the bush outside the window.

You're a small feather, winged seed, wisp
of cotton. Thread yourself
through a hole in the button on the sill.

You're a strand of dark thread
stitching a word to a river. Then another.

(kitchens)

Hirshfield - like

her ARS poetica

19

II.

Turned Sparrow

When geese lift away
to stitch the domed sky
when leaves loosen and fly
like charcoal wrens
when smoke tears from stacks like rags

then I remember my birth
my mother the rippling sky
measured by weather and wings
and me torn clear like a leaf
turned sparrow in a hard wind.

← previous

I swear it "stitch"
I'm back with kitchen
2 poems ago

balance of end line emphasis
with enjambments

In Which All Is Made Clear

Dragonfly gleam at selvage
of day, evening outskirts.
After the 7:30 whistle,
before the tracks begin their shudder

under an ear. There.
Next, pickpocket moon
makes off with meaning,
scribbles alibis across what turns

out to be an unreliable
horizon. Earlier, the shadows
implied another hemisphere,
perhaps a different sun?

Later, a child will dream
you watching her. The music
she hears—that's your latitude,
your ration of dawn for now.

These poems are so
dense, and so open outside
the window frame, stopping
to savor is called for

24

Burnished Way

Over the sea
the moon rides off
in a carriage
of clouds

Some nights
from a broken wave
silver lace
on onyx

Sometimes
under a strange pier
nest of embers
in the sand

Some darknesses
the burnished way   ) o—my—god   ✳
through waves
to the vessel of light

The speaker ear/mind
Gunpowder is fulfilling...

Time Travel
after Philip Larkin

Stumbling back to bed after a spell
out on the porch to still my leaping mind
I found that I was elsewhere altogether,
a house that I had lived in as a child.

And it was clear my sisters were there too
sleeping young and smooth beneath their sheets,
our brother in the next room calling out
Who's there? into the briefly simple dark.

Safe

I am six. I don't like coffee,
but the smell of it drifting
up the stairs
along with breakfast-making clatter
            means I'm safe.
                        I lie in bed, point
my toes, think about the secret
language I'm making, my list
of words and their meanings.
Today I'll write them in the book
I plan to make with sheets
of my mother's onion skin
            typing paper.
                        The summer I turn
nine, my father will find
a bat, rust-colored and furred,
roosting among the loquats
in our back yard. The breathing
fact of a wild creature so near
            will alarm and thrill me.
                        By then, my private
language will be forgotten,
not to be remembered until
I'm forty and look back to glimpse
myself in the amber
            wilds of my childhood,
first and last speaker
            of a snatch of language
                        without a name.

27

Beach Bone

Home with the evening's
haul of stones, a small
bone.

I like its slim curve,
first letter
of my name,

its smooth
bleached face,
weight of air.

It keeps its history,
this bone, and I approve
the mysteries

to which it won't allude.
It's here now in my
palm. That only.

(Tragedian ...)

"Aristotle said, 'The most
tragic ... Euripides ...)

V of Geese

V of geese above the house at dawn
slim moon dissolving into light

quiet the voices in the rafters
long enough for now

to be nothing else.

Then they start again
many versions of a single story.

See how the one you turn from
turns out to be what will not let you go.

Homage to Old Library Books and Childhood

Between pebbled covers
chapters sway like lanterns,
break like waves.

The librarian smoking
in the crow's nest
date-stamps every sorrow

for the next new moon,
every penny for the island
up ahead. We pass

the tin spyglass, scan
the purple ocean's sill, carve
our charts on soap,

rhyme our plans. And now
the shred of russet flag,
the enigmatic wake.

leaping

An Algebra of Fifty

Out back between the marvelous
weeds and the volunteer tomatoes,
she's a windsock in mid-life's rush
hour breeze. Day shuts down
all over. One plus n equals
match strike, doorbell, hush

of the crowd. Voices through
a window across a canyon, voices
across water, crickets in the ivy.
Anise seed on the tongue—texture,
then taste. Regret—taste, then
texture. A letter being opened
in Lisbon. Or not being opened

in the next room. Not the idea of God,
after all, nor God's proximity,
but the light under a door.
The breeze picks up, makes a nest
of her hair, as she solves for n
with all she's got. Behind her, the moon
rises burly, gibbous. The edges
of everything whistle.

enjambments

enjambments like
Nerothy's Tu Fu

* (

Some poets make you want
to write the instant the words
hit your eyes

31

Remembering Wind

This morning the air is still,
sky the color of tea
pouring. We remind
each other of the wind
    that woke us in the night
    called us outside

where it seemed only the stars
were standing still
    the stars and us
though of course we were in motion
and the stars at their far windows
had already gone dark.

III.

Instead of Sadness

I'm lying in the bathtub
thinking about death, land
that welcomes every immigrant,
no questions asked. No quotas,
no wall along the border.

More and more of those I love,
not to mention acquaintances
and people I've only read about
or seen on the news, have packed
nothing and moved there.

But I don't know.
I have what's probably
an irrational devotion to the mess
I'm in right here, a lot of which
I've made with my own hands.

And I would miss my books, a couple
of movies from the '90s, dollar stores.

All I'm saying is I think it warrants
further thought.

Something tells me, though, I'll meet
you there sooner or later. (You know
my famous hunches. Remember
Escondido? The green Volkswagen?)

I hear the wine is good—
that's something. Word gets back.

We'll find ourselves a rock in the sun,
take turns reciting Berryman
and Keats, maybe some Spender.
You can do a little Dylan
when the mood strikes.

For now, though, it's a jumbled
life: shabby, incandescent.
From the bathtub, through the window,
I can watch the stars come out.

Everything Important

happens behind my back.
Water lilies open, then close.
Nations are born. Friends up and leave
their sturdy bodies. The stonechat takes flight.
A son learns to whistle. A daughter finds
the greatest common factor, then falls
in love. One morning the leaves
are off the elm and halfway down the block.
And in the spring, however faithfully I check
for the first bloom along the secret alley
of camellias, I will be looking away,
will see them only once they're a jostling palaver
of pink and white, so impossible a brightness
I will forget to be disappointed.

Another Country

In the silence once
the sprinkler shuts off, a glaze
on the sidewalk.

Soon the sun will shrink it
to a damp shadow,
then nothing.

For now, another country,
familiar and strange,
shimmers there.

She's not going to be a great
writer someday.
This, what you're holding —
put your forehead
to the earth & it.

The Baptizer

Before it started I began to know
and then I knew. I wouldn't call it pleasure,
but there was satisfaction in the unfolding, a job
to do that I did, honey's wildness
a kind of welcome sting,
even the grasshoppers—strange elation
of eating a plague, being the devourer.

I comforted the wretched, my partner water,
found myself accuser of the mighty,
the comfortable. This too felt
good once I'd finished with fear.

There was a rhythm to it. It got so I knew
what would happen, who would come
before the day began,
how it would go.

The day he came, I knew
how that would go too, more surely than I'd known
anything yet, and then it didn't.

Under the Pier

Stand beneath the pier and look straight up. Daylight
      slats, strange colors, your life in ribbons
            will sting your eyes, stain your face, suggest
translations of your errand
      in this slim
            salted shadow.

January Song

The holidays are over. Now we're here
amidst the candle stubs and bits of ribbon.
Perhaps this stillness is a new career.

The kids had risen early, packed their gear,
made their farewells and then away they'd driven.
The holidays are over. We're still here

after waving from the porch as from a pier
at little crafts on course for the horizon.
Perhaps this stillness is a new career.

Time's origami has its way with fear,
with loss, bright things gone dark and plans gone riven.
The holidays are over. We're left here,

our failures folded into something dear
and strange and new, for which we haven't striven.
This stillness may become a new career.

Old age is coming, but it's not yet near.
These early afterhours are their own heaven.
A certain party's over; now we're here.
Today this stillness is a new career.

villanelle

Ash Wednesday Morning

The fat candle in the kitchen window burns down
like a rose spilling open. We light a scrap of paper
from the flame, and with the ashes, a little olive oil,
cross each other's foreheads. Margo's in the hospital
again. I stop to see her on my way to school,
go straight from there to class. My students have come
from their night shifts at the nursing home
and Wal-Mart, from Mass, from dropping off the baby
at daycare. They shuffle pages, share staplers.
We look into each other's faces as they hand me their essays.
Who knows how long we've got inside these dusty skins.
We're burning down together, ashes mingling already.

Legends of Quick

Cut to it. It and the dead.
Jack be nimble, Jack be
it. Jack taste the bloomy
wow of being and time's
sparrowed sky: what

we have of them,
who with. O
pronoun and preposition,
O ink smudge, eye-

lash, largesse of small
things, wink and pluck
of them, sparkle and muck

of it all, us all,
vaulting

the candlestick.

Compline

Before the carpet,
O my soul, before the carpet
lay down on the stone,
my life sat up inside my ribs
by candlelight,
said: *Listen*
for once.

As it was in the beginning,
is now and ever shall be,
world without end.

When the last note
finished ringing, when flames
were out, wicks cold,
I walked out under oaks
into a chapter house
of dying stars, new song
I knew by heart, by bone.

✝

I will never be the same
as in meeting merwin,
corsica, rille, michado
and the chinese

[No last lines to delete —
as in even Harrison and
william merwin]

Laying on of Hands

Small sycamore hands unfold
with or without our attention,
cupped in merry green possession

of what might be all we need.
They deck their trees like stars
deep into December.

Later, their sueded older selves
amble down the air
in big unpracticed cartwheels

(they only get one go),
then settle with a murmur,
a long, fond sigh:

a thousand starry hands
set down in blessing
on the round, bewildered world.

The restraint

IV.

Fallaway Rising

In the stony dawn the leavings start.
First the dreams. They rise or fall away,
leave filaments, crumbs, a feeling
someone tries to name for years.

At dawn the stony filaments of dreams
rise up to crumb the trusted tablecloth
until the leafy feeling falls away
until a name goes risen like a hill

unless the filamented falling dawn
unless the startled cloth rises again
to leave a feeling years of hills
will know as *dawncrumb, dreamleaf.*

In the naming stone a someone starts.
In the leaving feeling dreams the stone.

Little Web

Someone's shaken pollen
into the little web. You suspect
the sunflower, though it's hard
to think straight, hard

to do anything but go back
to sleep and finish the dream
over which, like the wind or love's
decedents, you have no control.

Just so with the spider, the pollen.
Love's a free fall, time's a fable,
love's the only time you've got.

The Boys Next Door

A few weeks back the boys next door named two of our sunflowers
after themselves. They like to check on their namesakes
late afternoons before bath time.

Both blooms are soaring now, having hit a growth spurt the last few days.
The boys stand close to the stalks, tilt their heads far back. These
are miracles. Overhead, the haloed faces blaze.

My Daughter and I Sleep in My Childhood Bedroom

Sometime after midnight, we wake
to a scritch and scuttle. Mice, I think, and traps.
Then a trilling question from the window
and we both turn our faces,

see two young raccoons pressed to the glass
regarding us with shining eyes. Our fingers touch;
we make small sounds of surprise. The kits pace the deep
sill, chatter in clear tones,

gazes never leaving us until they turn
and disappear down a branch into the dark. My daughter's
breathing slows at last to sleep. Moonlight makes
her cold migration through the room.

Something to Fill

Then said Jesus unto him,
"Except ye see signs and wonders,
ye will not believe."
                    John 4:48

I sat in the grass
bent over words
when slap into the stillness
flapped a mockingbird,

proclaimed the cherries ripe
by falling to.
That bird has an eye
for the delicious,

the signed and wondrous
moment that's gone
even as it arrives.
I spilled my pages, ran

for a bucket, a bowl,
something to fill.

There Should Be a Word

for the morning your daughter
comes home from college
for her friend's mom's
funeral, for how all
you know to do
is bake oatmeal bread,
for how the dough holds
its own against your palms

before it sighs in the pans.
For the flare of song
from a passing car, heartless
sunlight falling through the window,
playing on your skin, along the floor.
Your daughter in her bedroom
down the hall, the chiming
of the hangers through the wall.

She's condensed the forms,
Sr...u..., ses...i..., vill...n...ll...)
pm too...

Word. Phrase. Poem.

Does it create
like the bee at the sage
its own small wind?

Like the ant, does it carry
something larger than itself
without swaggering?

Letters from Birds

My first grade teacher told me
                feathers are letters from birds.
                                About that time I knew a lady

who wouldn't let her children
                touch feathers. They can
                                make you sick, she told them.

No, no! I wanted to shout, but
                I was small and she was big. I wanted
                        to tell her that feathers

are letters from birds, and letters
                are made of words, and words
                                (even then I knew this) words
                                  can make you well.

(all)

True and Useful

Morning flew in white and cool,
riff of feathered song.
And what were you to do
with your fantastic dram of fears

but tip the cup, spill them out,
watch them slip away to take
their true and useful places
in the halls of shuffled leaves:

dusty, dappled, going to earth.

Guilty of Dust
after George Herbert

As charged. It's everywhere, silent
witness to a fulsome sloth,
set to besmirch a glove
of any description.

It's a simple guilt,
one that may yet lead to repentance,
taking up of flannel cloths,
consecrating of lemon-scented oils,
beating of couch cushions.

What, though, of one guilty
less of sloth than wonder?

Think of it! The omnipresence
of dust, its democratic essence, grave
and twinkling persistence
in a hostile land and the interiors,
the very cupboards,
thereof.

Surely, Dust of Ages,
you're in cahoots (or should be)
with the Holy Ghost.

I wrap my complicated guilt about me
like a beaded cloak, then let it slip,
feel it fall, hear it pool at my feet.
Stand heretical, devout
in the sacrament
of your opal motes.

Last Night's Words

Awake at four a.m. to the ocean arguing
with the Lord again and in the waves
a silver tumble of words too many to catch
in such a dreamy net, I in my pajamas
and so far out.

As for morning,
sunlight poured down
honeylike, and tangled in the seaweed,
hiding from heroes, winking at children,
little stash of last night's words.

Beached now, they were chipped, scruffy
aubergines and rusts, small gleams.
Here is where I bend, select the strangest.
Here's where I kneel, rest my forehead
on the sand.

Anniversary

You uncork the wine and bring
your closing argument: the cerulean
interior of one of the delicate crab shells
you found on the beach. Even if you

weren't preaching to the choir,
I'd concede the point with pleasure
under the influence of that secret
blue. But do you see

the slightly different
shade inside the second shell, nested
now with precise tenderness
within the first? We'll call this one

Matchstrike, Fierce October, Time's Honest
Eye. These not-quite-twin astonishments:
they're *my* point, which takes yours
as its premise. Here's to love.

***

The morning after, and as if I'd thought
(which I did not) nothing could surprise me:

both blues have disappeared.
No by your leave, just up and gone,
and in their stead, two quaint shades of rose.

Yet even this we might have been expecting.
For where did our young faces go? Our babies
and your parents? What's a vanished
blue or two in our litany of losses.

***

Tonight I find another crab shell in your breast
pocket, smaller than the other two,

bleached as old bones on a strange
shore, secret as your brow in sleep.

Ways to Go

It's that October day when every elm's
a lantern, good thing in light
of the darkness.

Wildfires in California, 850,000 evacuated.
It looks like the end of the world
a man tells CNN.

And the world's end is the belly of the mountain
for the miners trapped inside, for their children,
parents, wives.

What my student's father calls to say,
words gone missing in his wrecked voice.

This afternoon's prognosis.

Worlds end every moment, and these elms
will dim. But today they pour light,
say there are ways to go, ways,
even, to go up in flames.

enter the breathing way
of Joy Harjo... (see Part poems)

V.

Dark and Late

This dark porch
has brimmed
with light
like a bowl with water
like a throat with laughter

afternoons of light
years of afternoons
scintillating dawns
flagrant noons
underwater-green dusks

and nights
dark and late
lit by candles, hands,
eyes with the leap
that's the life
we've come for,
what we carry
nonchalant
white-knuckled
down the spill of years,
what carries us, what
meets us in the end
and on the way
in each other.

Formal Nest

The bird I startled
just above your door—
above and to the left
and neatly hid
until a startler
of this stripe or that
makes her rude entrance
just the way I did—

that bird, I mean to say,
seems to have made
her second life in me
and plied her trade
the livelong yester-
day, well into night,
weaving a formal nest
of words and light.

Between Shores

Here in what I imagine
the middle of my life
the lake is rising.

Kingfisher signs a fleeting equator
across this morning's
page of world.

Egret, mid-flight
between shores, looks down
on an uncharted island

      quarter-
    acre of hyacinths
rafted together in last
     night's storm.

I taste her mild surprise,
quickened appetite,
watch her unscheduled descent.

She lands in the fish-rich tangle,
folds her wings.

Couch on the Beach

Someone dragged a hide-a-bed
onto the sand last night.
This morning there it sits, empty
as an open clam, clearly

slept in, face to face
with the Pacific. Less graceful
than a Massey-Ferguson
and less expected. Even the dogs,

after marking it theirs,
shake their heads. Still,
I recognize the impulse, the urge
to reach the furthest edge,

west of west, press up so close
and hard to beauty that it surges in,
then sweeps me new and desolate,
then enters me again.

Button Weather

Yesterday I sat
sewing buttons
on your shirt on the porch in the wind.
Afternoon clicked and thrummed. The shirt
                    whipped open like a spinnaker.
I squinted at my needle, domestic
in a gale.

my smile is ten thousand miles wide,
with two tears approaching.

Our Lady of Betwixt

She's the windowpane
greasy bloom of dust on glass
stunned bird in the dirt

splayed in the space

between this world (clocks
and creeks, nests of muddy lace)
and the next.

How the Soul Feels
after Dante Gabriel Rossetti

Like a rowboat of wet sand
at pond's edge in September.
Like a feather on that pond
and the ripples that run
all the way to shore.
It feels sequined,
seared, alight, aloft.
Feels like a song
you remember
from another life, then recall
composing. Like an ear
pressed to the heart
of an hour inside the one
you live now.

To quote...

Poets who can do this,
Tom Hennen
Betsy Sparks
Jane Hirshfield
Dan Gerber

Mary Jordan
to chu i

4 a Shu

71

South of Cayucos

I want to be that sheen
at low tide where the creek
meets the sea.

You wouldn't know
the place unless
you knew that creek,
unless you'd been there—
other tides, higher ones—
seen the flow cut
deep, the sandy banks
collapse again and again.

I want to be that shining skin
at lowest tide, sweet, salt,
moment of vanishing.

Hen Shen

pair this poems

H.S. p 57

in HJ. p 34

(Hilton
Wang wei)
p 59

(mourning Meng Hao-Jan)
my dear friend nowhere in sight,
this Han River keeps flowing east.
now if I look for old masters here,
a find empty rivers and mountains]
Wang wei.

Hamlet

on slender accident ..

when joy most revels
        grief doth most lament
grief joys, joy grieves, on
            slender accident
            — Hamlet

AUTHOR'S NOTES

"How to Begin": The "winged seed" arrived in this poem from Percy Bysshe Shelley's "Ode to the West Wind" via Thomas Merton's *New Seeds of Contemplation* and Li-Young Lee's memoir by that name.

"Compline": The lines "Before the carpet, / O my soul, before the carpet / lay down on the stone" refer to the years before the administration building at the University of Redlands was carpeted. The Chapel Singers, under the direction of Jeff Rickard, sang the office of Compline in that acoustically miraculous space.

"Last Night's Words": The second stanza plays with phrases from Leonard Cohen's song "Suzanne."

"Compline" is for Jeffrey H. Rickard.

"Formal Nest" is for John and Muriel Ridland.

"South of Cayucos" is for Karen Gookin.

My thanks to John and Muriel Ridland and Paul and Sharon Willis for long friendship in and out of poetry; to Melissa Martell Black, whose suggestions strengthened many of these poems; to my students and colleagues at Porterville College, and Andy Messchaert in memorium: thanks every day for your generosity and inspiration.

While in many ways teaching and poem-making are complementary endeavors, they can at times be (or at least seem) inimical to each other. In my efforts to maintain balance, I have been sustained by the fellowship and stimulation of weeks at the Napa Valley Writers Conference and the Blue Flower Arts Workshop at the Atlantic Center for the Arts. A number of the poems began, and others were revised, during a month of solitude at Tina Sheffield's Cayucos cottage.

Thanks forever to my parents, who kept an open dictionary within arm's reach of the dining table; to my siblings Russell, Anna, and Mim, for our life together then; and to Rob, Clara, and Mac, for our life together now.

To Dan Gerber for selecting the manuscript and to David Starkey, Chryss Yost, and Gunpowder Press for publishing it, deep gratitude.

About the Poet

Catherine Abbey Hodges is the author of the chapbook *All the While* (Finishing Line Press, 2006), a finalist in the New Women's Voices competition. Her poems have appeared in print and online journals including *The Southern Review*, *Tar River Poetry*, *Cider Press Review*, *Askew*, *Connotation Press*, *Christian Century*, and *Verse Daily*. She serves as a mentor to other writers and has led poetry workshops for adults and children.

A native of California, Hodges lived on the island of Sumatra in Indonesia for eight years with her husband Rob and their children, Clara and Mac. Currently at home in California's San Joaquin Valley, she teaches English at Porterville College, where she was named Faculty of the Year in 2009, and collaborates with musician Rob Hodges. For more information, visit www.linesandmeasures.com.

While reading these poems you
know the knowing is arriving
where you are awakening
you've never been - (or)
where you've been waiting for
your sleepy ½ self to
wake up to

CPSIA information can be obtained
at www.ICGtesting.com
Printed in the USA
FSOW01n0100291115
13845FS